MW00770725

SIMPLE THEOLOGY

SIMPLE
THEOLOGY

A GOSPEL CATECHISM
FOR KIDS

Written and Adapted By
DALE PARTRIDGE

Relearn Press
PRESCOTT, ARIZONA

© 2023 by Relearn.org. All rights reserved.

No portion of this book may be reproduced, stored in a retrieval system, or transmitted in any form or by any means— electronic, mechanical, photocopy, recording, scanning, or other—except for brief quotations in critical reviews or articles, without the prior written permission of the publisher.

Simple Theology: A Gospel Catechism for Kids
Published in Prescott, Arizona by Relearn.org
Written and Adapted by Dale Partridge
First Edition
ISBN: 979-8-9857492-6-7
Cover and Interior Illustrations: Adam Grason

Scripture quotations are from The ESV® Bible (The Holy Bible, English Standard Version®), copyright © 2001 by Crossway, a publishing ministry of Good News Publishers. Used by permission. All rights reserved.

Relearn Press is the publishing division of
Relearn.org. For information, please contact us through our website at Relearn.org.

To the parents who tirelessly labor to raise
their children in the knowledge and love of
Christ, dedicating their lives to instilling a deep
understanding of His lordship, His saving grace, and
His reign as King. You are the champions of gospel
fluency, equipping your families to engage the culture
with the transformative power of the cross.

Our Ministry

The mission of Relearn.org is simple:
To bring the church back to the Bible.
This is the driving force behind each of our
books, digital products, and podcasts.

Our Companion Ministries

Relearn.org
KingsWayBible.org
MailTheGospel.org
ReformationSeminary.com
StandInVictory.org
UltimateMarriage.com

Download Our App

Relearn.org/App

Table *of* Contents

WHY CATECHIZE YOUR CHILDREN?

Catechizing your child in the foundations of the faith when they are young will allow for greater comprehension of the deep things of God when they are grown.

A catechism is a collection of questions and answers that produce an orderly comprehension of biblical truths. Historically, catechism is an oral tradition where the instructor asks a list of particular questions, and the student memorizes and recites their answers. Most catechisms are connected to a specific confession of faith. For example, the *Westminster Confession of Faith* offers the accompanying *Shorter and Larger Catechism.* However, other catechisms like *The Heidelberg Catechism* are independent but hold strictly to reformed Protestant doctrine.

The word "catechism" is derived from the original Greek word *katecheo* (i.e., to teach orally, to instruct). The term is actually

1

found several times in the New Testament, including Luke 1:4, 1 Corinthians 14:19, Galatians 6:6, and Acts 18:25. Ultimately, catechism is a systematic approach to teaching doctrine to both children and adults.

Now, as a father of four children, I understand how difficult it can be to make time for family devotion and theological training. But the faithful commitment of a father or mother to catechize their children will be one of the most fruitful labors of their life. Overcoming the desire to abdicate this duty is often connected to vision. Today, we live in what's called the "Information Age." A time when children are bombarded with scores of ideas, viewpoints, worldviews, and philosophies. Charles Spurgeon famously said, "Whether we teach young Christians truth or not, the devil will be sure to teach them error."

As parents, we passionately train our kids in piano, sport, and art. We educate them in literature, history, and math. We pass on to them the wisdom of obedience and respect. While these are essential disciplines for life, they are nowhere near the importance of imparting the essentials of the Gospel.

Ephesians 6:4 tells fathers (and I would argue mothers, too) to "bring your children up in the discipline and instruction of the Lord." In the Old Testament, we see this intentional discipleship commanded in Deuteronomy 6:6–9. It says, "And these words that I command you today shall be on your heart. You shall teach them diligently to your children, and shall talk of them when you sit in your house, and when you walk by the way, and when you lie down, and when you rise. You shall bind them as a sign on your hand, and they shall be as frontlets between your eyes. You shall write them on the doorposts of your house and on your gates." In other words, the truth of God should saturate your house, lifestyle, and thoughts. Jesus, when asked which is the greatest commandment, answered, "You shall love the Lord your God with all your heart and with all your soul and with *all your mind*." I have italicized that last phrase because I want to emphasize the intellectual call to know God with our heads (and not just our hearts). All of these commands are surely fulfilled in the catechism of children.

But more than that, catechism sets a trajectory for spiritual and theological maturity that will leave them prepared for the more glorious truths of Scripture. It does this because catechism doesn't simply work on the memorization of particular Scriptures (which is also vital), but it teaches the meaning, theological significance, and application of the Scriptures.

Ultimately, catechism is the faithful act of passing down Christ to future generations. It is the fruitful side of God's command to be fruitful and multiply. It is, in a real sense, a form of evangelism and missional work for Christian homes. So, while it may be difficult and patient work, it is obedient work that lays critical foundations and glorifies God for generations to come.

After taking my children through several of the great historical catechisms, I noticed a few structural weaknesses that made them difficult to use.

As a result, I began making a list of ideas that could improve the process of catechism for the modern Christian family. Below are the three central problems we set out to solve:

1. There was no one-size-fits-all catechism. Namely, there were either catechisms for young children or catechisms for older children and adults. As a parent with children ranging from ten to newborn, I had to carry out two different catechisms, which was cumbersome and time-consuming. So, in *Simple Theology*, we have provided three different answer levels for each question to accommodate everyone from young children to adults. We have designed these levels around the theme of fruitfulness using the following titles:

1. **Seedlings** = Ages 3–7
2. **Sprouts** = Ages 8–11
3. **Vines** = Ages 12+

You will notice the answers for the Sprouts and Vines are in complete sentences, while the Seedling's responses are reduced to short statements for easier memorization.

2. Memorizing a complete catechism was very difficult. My children would memorize around 50–75 questions and answers, but retaining the answers to earlier questions was challenging when memorizing the answers to later questions. In addition, each night, it would take 5–15 minutes to work through the first 50+ questions before even getting to the later questions they still needed to hear and retain. This made catechism very time-consuming and, as a result, a daunting task for a busy parent.

For that reason, in *Simple Theology*, we have organized all 100 questions into seven blocks. Each block has between 5-20 questions. They are as follows:

HOW TO USE THIS CATECHISM?

Block #1: Gospel (20 Questions)

Block #2: Theology (20 Questions)

Block #3: Man (15 Questions)

Block #4: Law (15 Questions)

Block #5: Church (15 Questions)

Block #6: Worship (10 Questions)

Block #7: Evangelism (5 Questions)

After your child memorizes the questions within a certain block, they can take a verbal exam. If they pass, they can move on to the next block without the pressure to retain the answers to the previous block. We have found that families who catechize their children daily can memorize between 2–10 questions per week. That said, it's not uncommon for it to take 6–12 months for a child to complete this catechism.

Remember, discipleship is not a race. Memorization is the goal, and if their mind has achieved that goal, these truths will be retained (to some degree), forever shaping the way they think about God, themselves, and the Gospel. Can you work with your child to memorize the entire catechism within their level? Absolutely! In fact, we encourage you to do so. If your child accomplishes this feat, we have a free certificate you can print out at Relearn.org/Certificate.

3. The catechisms of the past were fiercely denominational.
That is, *The Westminster Shorter Catechism*, *The Baptist Catechism*, and *The Heidelberg Catechism* were quite aggressive toward the views of the other catechisms. This was mainly around the issues of baptism, the Lord's Supper, and church government. However, our ministry is a strong proponent of what is called "reformed catholicity." Namely, we aim to unify and honor any denomination that stands by the great reformed confessions of faith (e.g., *The Westminster Confession*, *The 1689 London Baptist Confession*, *The Belgic Confession*, etc.). So, in *Simple Theology*, you will see answers around those more controversial issues that are acceptable to all within the Reformed Protestant tradition.

Ultimately, we believe if a catechism is beautiful, fun, and easy to use, more parents will use it, and more children will enjoy it. As a result, God will save His people. This is the hope behind our efforts at Relearn.org and in the Relearn App. May God bless your faithful efforts.

To Him be the glory,

Dale Partridge
Prescott, Arizona, 2023

DISCLAIMER

Several of these questions and answers are not originally written content but collected, adapted, edited, or modernized versions of questions and answers from historic Christian catechisms.

GOSPEL

Block 01 • Questions 1–20

What do the icons represent?

Simple Theology caters to individuals of all ages by providing three answer levels per question: complete sentences for Sprouts and Vines, and concise statements for easier memorization by Seedlings.

 Seedlings = Ages 3–7

 Sprouts = Ages 8-11

 Vines = Ages 12+

What is your only comfort in life and death?

 That I am not my own, but my body and soul belong to Jesus Christ.

 My only comfort is that, as a Christian, I am not my own, but my body and soul belong to my Savior, Jesus Christ, who died for my sins and rose from the grave to save me from the wrath of God.

 My only comfort in life and death is that, as a Christian, I am not my own, but belong with body and soul, both in life and in death, to my Savior Jesus Christ; who has paid for all my sins with his blood and accomplished victory over death by his resurrection, thereby saving me from the wrath of God.

REFERENCES

Acts 26:18; 1 Cor. 6:19, 20; 15:3–4; Rom. 4:24–25; 5:9; 14:7-9; 1 Cor. 3:23; Tit. 2:14; 1 Pet. 1:18; 19; 1 John 1:7; 2:2; John 8:34-36; Heb. 2:14, 15; 1 John 3:8.

"The Lord is my light and my salvation;
whom shall I fear?"

PSALM 27:1

What do you need to know to live and die in this comfort?

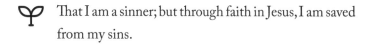 That I am a sinner; but through faith in Jesus, I am saved from my sins.

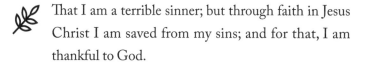 That I am a terrible sinner; but through faith in Jesus Christ I am saved from my sins; and for that, I am thankful to God.

That I am a terrible sinner; but through faith in Jesus Christ I am saved from the condemnation of my sins against God and His Law; and for that, I must remain thankful to God for my deliverance.

REFERENCES

Rom. 3:9, 10; 1 John 1:10; John 17:3; Acts 4:12; 10:43; Matt. 5:16; Rom. 6:13; Eph. 5:8-10; 1 Pet. 2:9, 10.

SCRIPTURE: 1 JOHN 1:9

"If we confess our sins, he is faithful and just to forgive us our sins and to cleanse us from all unrighteousness."

What condemns you as a terrible sinner?

 The Ten Commandments.

 The Ten Commandments—often called the Moral Law of God.

 The Ten Commandments—often called the Moral Law, which were delivered to Moses by God on Mt. Sinai.

REFERENCES

Exod. 20; Rom. 3:10–18; 3:20; 4:15; 5:20; 7:7–25; 1 Cor. 15:56; Gal. 3:19; 1 Tim. 1:8–11.

SCRIPTURE: JAMES 2:10

"For whoever keeps the whole law but fails in one point has become guilty of all of it."

Can you keep the
Ten Commandments perfectly?

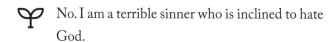

No. I am a terrible sinner who is inclined to hate God.

No. I am a terrible sinner who is inclined to hate God, hate others, and love myself.

No. I am a terrible sinner with a sinful nature that is inclined to hate God, hate others, and love myself.

REFERENCES

Rom. 3:10, 23; 1 John 1:8, 10; Gen. 6:5; 8:21; Jer. 17:9; Rom. 7:23; 8:7; Eph. 2:3; Tit. 3:3.

SCRIPTURE: ROMANS 3:23

"For all have sinned and fall short of the glory of God."

Did God create humans as terrible sinners?

 No. God created mankind sinless, so they might remain in His presence.

 No. God created mankind sinless and in His image so humanity might know Him and remain in His presence.

 No. God created Adam and Eve in His image as sinless, holy, and righteous so humanity might rightly know God and remain in His presence and glorify Him forever.

REFERENCES
Gen. 1:31, 1:26, 27; Eph. 4:24; Col. 3:10; Ps. 8.

SCRIPTURE: GENESIS 1:31
"And God saw everything that he had made, and behold, it was very good."

How did sin enter the world?

 Through Adam and Eve's disobedience to God.

 Sin entered the world through Adam and Eve's disobedience to God, plunging themselves and all their descendants into sin.

 Sin entered the world through our first parents, Adam and Eve, when they disobeyed God, plunging themselves and their descendants into sin, corrupting their nature, making them unrighteous, and separating themselves from God.

REFERENCES
Gen. 3; Rom. 5:12, 18, 19; Ps. 51:5.

SCRIPTURE: GENESIS 3:24
"He drove out the man, and at the east of the garden of Eden he placed the cherubim and a flaming sword that turned every way to guard the way to the tree of life."

How did you become such a terrible sinner?

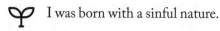 I was born with a sinful nature.

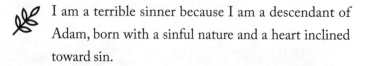 I am a terrible sinner because I am a descendant of Adam, born with a sinful nature and a heart inclined toward sin.

I am a terrible sinner because I am a descendant of Adam who sinned against God and inherited his sinful nature. Without redemption, my heart will continue to love sin.

REFERENCES

Gen. 6:5; Jer. 17:9; Hos. 6:7; Mark 7:21–23; Rom. 5:12–21; 1 Cor. 15:22; 2 Cor. 4:3–4.

SCRIPTURE: ROMANS 5:19

"For as by the one man's disobedience the many were made sinners."

Will God allow your sin to go unpunished?

 No. God is angry with all my sin and will punish sinners with eternal consequences.

 No. God is angry with my sinful nature and my acts of sin. He will judge sinners by His Law and punish them with eternal consequences.

 No. God is angry with my sinful nature and my acts of sin. He will judge sinners by His Law and punish them with eternal consequences for their sins against an eternal God.

REFERENCES

Gen. 2:17; Exod. 34:7; Ps. 5:4-6; 7:11; Nah. 1:2; Rom. 1:18; 5:12; Eph. 5:6; Heb. 9:27; Deut. 27:26.

SCRIPTURE: GENESIS 3:24

"I will punish the world for its evil, and the wicked for their iniquity…"

But is God not a God of mercy?

God is just and merciful. He punishes sinners but also provides a Savior.

God is both just and merciful. His justice requires that sin must be punished, but His mercy is seen in providing His people with a Savior.

God is both just and merciful. His justice requires that sin must be punished, but His mercy is seen in providing a Savior who took the punishment for all who would turn from their sin and trust in Him alone.

REFERENCES
Exod. 20:6; 34:6, 7; Ps. 103:8, 9; Exod. 20:5; 34:7; Deut. 7:9-11; Ps. 5:4-6; Heb. 10:30, 31; Matt. 25:45, 46.

SCRIPTURE: LAMENTATIONS 3:22-33
"The steadfast love of the Lord never ceases; his mercies never come to an end; they are new every morning; great is your faithfulness."

What is the just punishment for your sins against a holy and eternal God?

 Physical and spiritual death.

 The just punishment for my sins is physical and spiritual death. Without redemption, my soul will be eternally separated from God, and this separation will be filled with torture, agony, and darkness.

 The just punishment for my sins against a holy and eternal God is physical and spiritual death. Without redemption, my physical body will be eternally separated from my soul, and my soul will be eternally separated from God. This just separation will be filled with torture, agony, and darkness.

REFERENCES

2 Thess. 1:8-9; Luke 16:24; Rev. 20:14–15; Matt. 8:12; 1 Pet. 3:19; Jude 1:13; Matt. 25:46; Heb. 9:27.

"For the wages of sin is death…"

ROMANS 6:23

Since God is a God of justice, can you avoid your eternal punishment and be reconciled to God?

 No. I must pay for my sins unless someone acts as my substitute.

 No. I must die an eternal death and make full payment for my sins unless payment is made by a sinless substitute on my behalf.

 No. Justice demands I must die an eternal death and make full payment for my sins unless payment is made by a perfect and sinless substitute who dies on my behalf.

REFERENCES

Exod. 20:5; 23:7; John 3:36; Rom. 2:1-11; Isa. 53:11; Rom. 8:3, 4; Revelation 20:11-15.

SCRIPTURE: HEBREWS 9:27

"And just as it is appointed for man to die once, and after that comes judgment..."

Who can act as a sinless substitute for you?

 Only another human who has no sin of their own.

 Only another human, born without sin, who lived under the Law without breaking it, making them sinless, can act as my sinless substitute.

 Only another human, born without sin, who lived under the Law of God, yet without breaking it, making them perfect and sinless, can act as my sinless substitute.

REFERENCES
Isa. 7:14; 9:6; 53:9; Jer. 23:6; John 1:1; Rom 5:12, 15; 8:3; 1 Cor. 15:21; 2 Cor. 5:21; Heb. 2:14–17; 7:26–27; 1 Pet. 3:18.

SCRIPTURE: HEBREWS 2:17
"Therefore He had to be made like His brothers in every respect, so that he might become a merciful and faithful high priest in the service of God, to make propitiation for the sins of the people."

Who is this sinless substitute who can satisfy the wrath of a holy God?

 The Man Jesus Christ—who alone was fully human and fully divine.

 The Man Jesus Christ—who alone was fully human and fully divine. His humanity made Him a substitute for human punishment, and His divinity made Him able to withstand and satisfy the wrath of God.

 The Man Jesus Christ—who alone was fully human and fully divine. His humanity made Him a substitute for human punishment, and His divinity made Him able to withstand and satisfy the wrath of God.

REFERENCES

Isa. 9:6, 53:5, 11; Deut. 4:24; Nah. 1:6; Ps. 130:3; John 3:16; 2 Cor. 5:21; Matt. 1:21-23; Luke 2:11; 1 Tim. 2:5; 3:16.

SCRIPTURE: 2 CORINTHIANS 5:21

"For our sake he made him to be sin who knew no sin, so that in him we might become the righteousness of God."

Where do you learn about the Lord Jesus Christ and His willingness to act as your substitute?

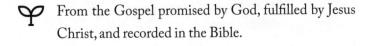 From the Gospel promised by God, fulfilled by Jesus Christ, and recorded in the Bible.

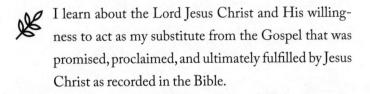 I learn about the Lord Jesus Christ and His willingness to act as my substitute from the Gospel that was promised, proclaimed, and ultimately fulfilled by Jesus Christ as recorded in the Bible.

I learn about the Lord Jesus Christ and His willingness to act as my substitute from the Gospel, which God first revealed and promised in the Garden of Eden, which was proclaimed by the patriarchs and prophets, foreshadowed by the ceremonial sacrifices of the Law, fulfilled by Jesus Christ Himself, and recorded for humanity in the Holy Bible.

REFERENCES

Luke 22:37; 24:25-27, 24:44–46; John 8:56–58, 20:30–

31; Acts 26:22–23; 1 Cor. 10:1–11; 1 Cor. 15:45; Heb. 1:1–2; 1 Pet. 1:10–12; Rev. 1:3.

SCRIPTURE: LUKE 24:25-27

"And he said to them, "O foolish ones, and slow of heart to believe all that the prophets have spoken! Was it not necessary that the Christ should suffer these things and enter into His glory?" And beginning with Moses and all the Prophets, he interpreted to them in all the Scriptures the things concerning Himself."

What substitutionary work did Jesus Christ accomplish for you?

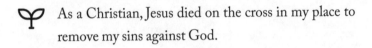 As a Christian, Jesus died on the cross in my place to remove my sins against God.

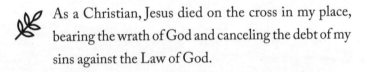 As a Christian, Jesus died on the cross in my place, bearing the wrath of God and canceling the debt of my sins against the Law of God.

As a Christian, Jesus died on the cross in my place, was forsaken by the Father, bore the wrath of God, and His blood atoned for my sin, canceling the debt of my sins against the Law of God, and granting me eternal peace with the Father.

REFERENCES
Lev. 17:11; Isa. 53:4–6, 10–12; Mark 10:45; John 1:29; Rom. 3:21–26, 5:1; 2 Cor. 5:21; Gal. 3:13–14; Col. 2:13–14; Heb. 9:11–12; 1 Pet. 2:24; 3:18.

SCRIPTURE: COLOSSIANS 2:13–14
"And you, who were dead in your trespasses and the

uncircumcision of your flesh, God made alive together with him, having forgiven us all our trespasses, by canceling the record of debt that stood against us with its legal demands. This he set aside, nailing it to the cross."

Why did Jesus have to die?

 To pay for the sins of His people.

 The Bible declares the wages of sin is death. Therefore, Jesus had to die for God's justice to be satisfied, and for the sins of His people to be forgiven.

 Jesus had to die because God's Word declares the wages of sin is death. Because Jesus was sinless, He died not for His sins but for the sins of His people, satisfying the justice and wrath of God and securing forgiveness for all who trust in Him.

REFERENCES
Isa. 53:4–5; John 4:34; 5:30; 6:38–39; Acts 26:63; Rom. 6:23; 2 Cor. 5:21; Gal. 3:13; Heb. 9:26.

SCRIPTURE: ISAIAH 53:5
"But he was pierced for our transgressions; he was crushed for our iniquities; upon him was the chastisement that brought us peace, and with his wounds we are healed."

How can Jesus Christ be applied as your substitute?

 Jesus Christ can be my substitute by having faith in Him alone.

 Jesus Christ can be my substitute when I repent of my sins and have faith in Jesus Christ alone.

 Jesus Christ can be my substitute when my sin so grieves my heart, and my soul is so fearful of God's judgment that I repent of my sins and have faith in Jesus Christ alone.

REFERENCES

John 3:5, 16–18, 36; Rom. 1:16–17; 3:21–26; 5:1; 10:10–13; Eph. 2:8–9; 1 Cor. 1:21; Gal. 2:16, 20.

SCRIPTURE: EPHESIANS 2:8-9

"For by grace you have been saved through faith. And this is not your own doing; it is the gift of God, not a result of works, so that no one may boast."

What do you have faith in Christ to do?

 To pay for my sins and give me His righteousness.

 I have faith that Christ paid the debt of my sins on the cross and gave me His righteousness making me not guilty before God.

 I have faith that Christ paid the debt of my sins through His atoning blood spilled at the cross and imputed His righteousness to me through faith, justifying me before God and allowing me to be found not guilty on Judgment Day.

REFERENCES
Matt. 9:2; 21:21; Luke 5:20; 7:50; 17:6; Acts 15:9; Rom. 1:17; 3:21–26; 1 Cor. 1:21; Gal. 2:16, 20; Eph. 2:8–9.

SCRIPTURE: GALATIANS 2:16
"Yet we know that a person is not justified by works of the law but through faith in Jesus Christ..."

Where does this saving faith come from?

 God, who gifts it to any person who hears and understands the Gospel.

 Saving faith is a gift of God delivered by the Holy Spirit to any person who hears and understands the Gospel of Jesus Christ.

 Saving faith is a gift of God delivered by the Holy Spirit to any person who hears and understands the Gospel of Jesus Christ. This faith cannot be lost and will be sustained by the Holy Spirit forever.

REFERENCES
Matt. 16:15–17; Acts 16:14; Rom. 3:21–26; 10:17; 1 Cor. 1:21; Eph. 2:8–9; Heb. 10:10.

SCRIPTURE: ROMANS 10:17
"So faith comes from hearing, and hearing through the Word of Christ."

What is essential for you to believe to call yourself Christian?

THE APOSTLES' CREED (FOR SEEDLINGS-VINES)

I believe in God the Father almighty,[1]
Creator of heaven and earth.[2]
I believe in Jesus Christ,
His only-begotten Son,[3] my Lord;[4]
He was conceived by the Holy Spirit,[5]
born of the virgin Mary;[6]
suffered under Pontius Pilate,[7]
was crucified,[8] dead,[9] and buried;[10]
He descended into hell.*
On the third day, He arose from the dead;[11]
He ascended into heaven,[12]
and sits at the right hand[13]
of God the Father almighty;
from there, He will come to judge
the living and the dead.[14]

I believe in the Holy Spirit;[15]
I believe a holy catholic* church,[16]

the communion of saints;[17]

the forgiveness of sins;[18]

the resurrection of the body;[19]

and the life everlasting.[20]

REFERENCES

[1]*Rev. 4:8;* [2]*Gen. 1:1;* [3]*Matt. 3:16–17;* [4]*Rom. 10:9;* [5]*Luke 1:34–35;* [6]*Matt. 1:18;* [7]*Mark 15:15;* [8]*Mark 15:25;* [9]*John 19:33–34;* [10]*Luke 23:52;* [11]*Luke 24:1–7;* [12]*Luke 24:51;* [13]*Col. 3:1;* [14]*2 Tim. 4:1;* [15]*John 14:26;* [16]*Gal. 3:26–29;* [17]*Heb. 10:25;* [18]*Luke 7:48;* [19]*1 Thess. 4:16;* [20]*John 10:28*

*There is a dispute among theologians over how this is stated. The statement is referencing concepts from Matthew 27:46 and Hebrews 13:11–12.

*The true universal Christian church of all times and all places.

BLOCK #1 GOSPEL: VERBAL EXAM

Parents, sit down with your child and joyfully examine their memorization of questions 1-20.

The aim is substantial memorization, not perfect memorization. Remember, there is no timeline for this exam to be completed. It may take one try or several. The goal is consistent and faithful mental discipleship until your child can recite and understand these questions and answers within their category (seedlings, sprouts, or vines).

Do not move on until your child has completed this Block exam. Once the exam is completed, your child no longer has to practice or recite the content within this Block and can move onto the memorization of the following Block.

THEOLOGY

What is the Holy Bible?

 The inspired and revealed Word of God.

 The Holy Bible is the inspired and revealed Word of God. It is perfect, without error, and in it holds all of God's authority to mankind.

 The Holy Bible is the inspired and revealed Word of God preserved in the 39 books of the Old Testament and 27 books of the New Testament. It is perfect, without error, and carries the weight of God's authority to mankind.

REFERENCES

Deut. 4:2; Ps. 19:7–11; 33:4; 119:105–112, 160; Prov. 30:5; Isa. 40:8; 55:11; Matt. 24:35; Luke 24:27, 44; John 1:1; 2 Tim. 3:15–17; Heb. 1:1–2; 4:12; 2 Pet. 1:20–21; 3:2.

SCRIPTURE: 2 TIMOTHY 3:16-17

"All Scripture is breathed out by God and profitable for teaching, for reproof, for correction, and for training in righteousness, that the man of God may be complete, equipped for every good work."

"All Scripture is breathed out by God and profitable for teaching, for reproof, for correction, and for training in righteousness, that the man of God may be complete, equipped for every good work."

2 TIMOTHY 3:16-17

What does the Bible principally teach?

 What humanity is to believe about God, ourselves, and the Gospel.

 The Bible principally teaches what humanity is to believe about God, ourselves, and the Gospel.

 The Bible principally teaches what humanity is to believe about God, ourselves, and the Gospel. It presents the truth about right and wrong, wisdom and foolishness, and guides us to holy living.

REFERENCES

Gen. 1:1; Deut. 10:12–13. Josh 1:8; Ps. 119:105; Mic. 6:8; John 5:39; 20:31; Rom. 10:17; 2 Tim. 3:15–17.

SCRIPTURE: 2 PETER 1:19-21

"And we have the prophetic word more fully confirmed, to which you will do well to pay attention as to a lamp shining in a dark place, until the day dawns and the morning star rises in your hearts, knowing this first of all, that no prophecy of Scripture comes from someone's own interpretation. For no prophecy was ever produced by the will of man, but men spoke from God as they were carried along by the Holy Spirit."

Who is God?

 God is the Creator. He is a Spirit and does not have a body like men.

 God is the eternal Creator of heaven and earth. He is a Spirit and does not have a body like men.

 God is the Creator of heaven and earth. He is a Spirit and does not have a body like men. He is infinite, eternal, and unchangeable. He is perfect love, wisdom, power, holiness, justice, mercy, goodness, and truth.

REFERENCES

Gen 1:1; 17:1; 18:25; Exod. 3:14; 34:6–7; Deut. 4:15–19; 32:4; 33:27; 1 Kings 8:27; Ps. 33:11; 62:11; 86:15; 90:2; 96:13; 102:12, 24–27; 103:5; 104:24; 107:8; 115:2–3; 117:2; 139:7–10; 145:3; 147:5; Jer. 23:24; 32:17; Mal. 3:6; Matt. 19:17, 26; Luke 24:39; John 1:18; 4:24; Acts 17:29; Rom. 2:4; 3:5, 26; 11:33–36; 1 Tim. 1:17; 6:15–16; Heb. 1:12–13; 4:13; 6:17–18; 13:8; Jas. 1:17; 1 Pet. 1:15–16; 1 John 3:3, 520; Rev. 1:4, 8; 15:4.

SCRIPTURE: 1 CHRONICLES 29:11-12

"Yours, O Lord, is the greatness and the power and the glory and the victory and the majesty, for all that is in the heavens and in the earth is yours. Yours is the kingdom, O Lord, and you are exalted as head above all. Both riches and honor come from you, and you rule over all. In your hand are power and might, and in your hand it is to make great and to give strength to all."

Is there more than one God?

 No. There is only one true and living God—His name is Yahweh.

 No. There is only one true and living God—His name is Yahweh. Anyone who claims there is more than one God has not read and understood the Bible.

 No. There is only one true and living God—His name is Yahweh. Anyone who claims there is more than one God has been deceived by demonic forces, religion, or the foolish philosophies of men. These people have not yet read and understood the Bible.

REFERENCES
Deut. 6:4; Isa. 44:6; 45:21-22; Jer. 10:10; John 17:3; 1 Cor. 8:4-6; 1 Thess. 1:9; 1 John 5:20.

SCRIPTURE: DEUTERONOMY 6:4
"Hear, O Israel: The Lord our God, the Lord is one."

How many persons are in this one God?

 Three. The Father, the Son, and the Holy Spirit.

 There are three persons in the Godhead; the Father, the Son, and the Holy Spirit, and these three are one God.

 There are three persons in the Godhead; the Father, the Son, and the Holy Spirit, and these three are one God, the same in essence, equal in power and glory.

REFERENCES

Ps. 45:6; Matt. 3:16-17; 28:19; John 1:1; 15:26; 17:5; Acts 2:33; Rom. 9:5; 2 Cor. 13:14; Eph. 2:18, 22; Col. 2:9; Heb. 9:14; 1 Pet. 1:2; Jude 24–25.

SCRIPTURE: 2 CORINTHIANS 13:14

"The grace of the Lord Jesus Christ and the love of God and the fellowship of the Holy Spirit be with you all."

When Christians speak of God, which Person of the Trinity are they referring to?

 God the Father.

 They are speaking of God the Father and His being, character, and attributes that have been revealed in Scripture.

 They are speaking of God the Father the first Person of the Trinity and His being, character, and attributes that have been revealed in Scripture.

REFERENCES

Ps. 68:5; Isa. 63:16; 64:8; Mal. 2:10; Matt. 6:9; 23:9; 1 Cor. 8:6; Eph. 4:6; Jas. 1:17; 1 John 3:1.

SCRIPTURE: ISAIAH 64:8

"But now, O Lord, you are our Father; we are the clay, and you are our potter; we are all the work of your hand."

Is God male or female?

 God is male.

 In Scripture, God is only presented as male. He is not female or genderless.

 In Scripture, God is only presented as male. He is not female or genderless. He is the perfect Father, eternally male and divinely masculine.

REFERENCES

Gen 1:5 (first masculine pronoun in the Bible), 27; Isa. 54:5; Matt. 6:9; John 20:17; Eph. 3:14–15; 1 Tim. 6:15.

SCRIPTURE: ISAIAH 54:5

"For your Maker is your husband, the Lord of hosts is his name; and the Holy One of Israel is your Redeemer, the God of the whole earth he is called."

What does it mean that God is sovereign?

 God is King and governs everything according to His rule.

 The sovereignty of God means that He is King over all creation, and He governs all things according to His perfect rule.

 The sovereignty of God means that He is King over all creation. He rightfully governs all things, and no action in life occurs without the intention or permission of His perfect rule.

REFERENCES

Job 42:2; Ps. 95:2–3, 6–7; 96:9–10; 135:6; Prov. 16:33; Isa. 45:7–9; Lam. 3:37–39; Matt. 10:29–31; Acts 4:27–28; Rom. 8:28; 11:36; Eph. 1:4, 11; Col. 1:16–17.

SCRIPTURE: ROMANS 11:36

"For from him and through him and to him are all things. To him be glory forever. Amen."

What does it mean that God is Omnipotent?

 God is all-powerful.

 The omnipotence of God means that God is all-powerful. He writes history, saves sinners, and accomplishes all His holy will.

 The omnipotence of God means that God is all-powerful. He cannot be controlled, prevented, or swayed. He writes history, saves sinners, and accomplishes all His holy will.

REFERENCES

Gen. 1:1; 18:14; 45:5–8; Exod. 4:21; Deut. 18:21–22; Ps. 105:24–25; 115:3; 135:6; 139:13–16; Prov. 16:33; Isa. 55:11; Jer. 32:17; Lam. 3:37–38; Matt. 6:26–30; 10:29–30; Acts 13:48; 16:14–15; Rom. 8:28; 9:18; 11:33–36; Eph. 1:11; 2:8–10; Jas. 4:13–17.

SCRIPTURE: 2 CORINTHIANS 13:14

"Whatever the Lord pleases, he does, in heaven and on earth, in the seas and all deeps."

What does it mean that God is Omniscient?

 God knows everything, and nothing can be hidden from Him.

 The omniscience of God means that God is all-knowing. He does not learn. He sees everything, and nothing can be hidden from Him.

 The omniscience of God means that God is all-knowing. He does not learn. He knows everything about Himself, His creation, history, and the future. He sees everything, and nothing can be hidden from Him.

REFERENCES
1 Sam. 10:2; 1 Kgs 13:1–4; 2 Kgs 8:12; Ps. 139:1–6; 147:5; John 21:17; Acts 2:23; 4:27–28; Heb. 4:12–13; 1 John 3:20.

SCRIPTURE: 1 JOHN 3:20
"For whenever our heart condemns us, God is greater than our heart, and he knows everything."

What does it mean that God is Omnipresent?

 God is always present everywhere.

 The omnipresence of God means that God is always present. There is no place or time where God is not.

 The omnipresence of God means that God is always present. As Creator and Sustainer of all things, He is in every place in every time. There is no place or time where God is not.

REFERENCES
Gen. 26:3; Exod. 6:7; Ps. 33:13–14; 139:7–10; Isa. 40:12; 57:15; 2 Cor. 6:16; Rev. 1:7.

SCRIPTURE: PSALM 139:7-10
"Where shall I go from your Spirit? Or where shall I flee from your presence? If I ascend to heaven, you are there! If I make my bed in Sheol, you are there! If I take the wings of the morning and dwell in the uttermost parts of the sea, even there your hand shall lead me..."

Who is Jesus Christ?

 The Lord, the Son of God, and the Savior of His people.

 Jesus Christ is Lord, the second Person of the Trinity, the eternal Son of God, and the Savior of His people.

 Jesus Christ is Lord, the second Person of the Trinity, the eternal Son of God, and the Savior of His people. He became man, born of a virgin, and remains God and man in two distinct natures found in one person.

REFERENCES

Ps. 2:7; Isa. 9:6; Matt. 1:21–23; 3:17; 17:5; 27:54; Luke 2:11; John 1:14, 18; 3:16; 14:6; Acts 1:11; 4:12; Gal. 4:4; 1 Tim. 2:5–6; 3:16; Heb. 1:1–4; 7:24–25.

SCRIPTURE: MATTHEW 27:54

"When the centurion and those who were with him, keeping watch over Jesus, saw the earthquake and what took place, they were filled with awe and said, 'Truly this was the Son of God!'"

"When the centurion and those who were with
him, keeping watch over Jesus, saw the earthquake
and what took place, they were filled with awe and
said, 'Truly this was the Son of God!'"

MATTHEW 27:54

What roles does Jesus Christ fulfill as Savior?

 Prophet, Priest, and King.

 As Savior, Jesus Christ fulfills the roles of Prophet, Priest, and King. As Prophet, He proclaims salvation. As Priest, He intercedes by sacrifice. As King, He conquerors sin.

 As Savior, Jesus Christ fulfills the roles of Prophet, Priest, and King. As Prophet, He revealed God's way of salvation. As Priest, He offered Himself as a sacrifice and intercedes for His people. As King, He rules and defends His church by conquering all His and her enemies.

REFERENCES
Deut. 18:15, 18; Isa. 9:6–7; Luke 1:32–33; John 18:37; Acts 2:33; 3:22-23; 1 Cor. 15:25; Heb. 1:1-2; 4:14–15; 5:5–6.

SCRIPTURE: HEBREWS 1:1-2
"Long ago, at many times and in many ways, God spoke to our fathers by the prophets, but in these last days he has spoken to us by his Son, whom he appointed the heir of all things, through whom also he created the world."

Where is Jesus Christ now?

 Sitting at the right hand of God, ruling the world.

 After His resurrection, Christ was exalted in His ascension as King and now sits at the right hand of God with all power and authority in heaven and on earth.

 After His resurrection, Christ was exalted in His ascension as King and now sits at the right hand of God with all power and authority in heaven and on earth, where He is building and defending His Church, conquering His enemies, and reigning until His second coming.

REFERENCES
Ps. 68:18; 110:1; Mark 16:19; Luke 24:50–51; Acts 1:9–11; 2:33–34; Rom. 8:34; 1 Cor. 15:4; Eph. 4:8; Heb. 1:3; 4:14; 7:23–25; 9:24.

SCRIPTURE: MARK 16:19
"So then the Lord Jesus, after he had spoken to them, was taken up into heaven and sat down at the right hand of God."

When will Jesus Christ return to the earth?

 When He Has redeemed all His people.

 Jesus Christ will return when He Has redeemed the last of His people through the fulfillment of the Great Commission.

 Jesus Christ will return when He Has redeemed the last of His people from every tribe, nation, and tongue through the fulfillment of the Great Commission.

REFERENCES

Matt. 16:27; 24:30, 36; 28:16–20; Mark 13:33; John 14:3; Acts 1:11; 17:31; Jas. 5:7.

SCRIPTURE: ACTS 17:31

"Because he has fixed a day on which he will judge the world in righteousness by a man whom he has appointed; and of this he has given assurance to all by raising him from the dead."

How will Jesus Christ
return to the earth?

 Visibly in His body for all to see.

 Christ will return dramatically, visibly, and bodily to the earth, and He will judge all men in righteousness.

 Christ will return dramatically, visibly, and bodily to the earth; the dead will be raised; and He will judge all men in righteousness. The unrighteous will be sent to Hell; The righteous in their resurrected and glorified bodies will receive their reward and will dwell forever with Christ upon the new heavens and earth.

REFERENCES
Matt. 16:27; 24:30, 36; Luke 11:2; John 14:3; Acts 1:11; 17:31; Jas. 5:7; Rev. 7:9–10.

SCRIPTURE: MATTHEW 24:30
"Then will appear in heaven the sign of the Son of Man, and then all the tribes of the earth will mourn, and they will see the Son of Man coming on the clouds of heaven with power and great glory."

Who is the Holy Spirit?

 The third Person of the Trinity, fully and truly God.

 The Holy Spirit is the third Person of the Trinity, fully and truly God, and is sent by the Father and the Son.

 The Holy Spirit is the third Person of the Trinity, fully and truly God, and eternally proceeding from the Father and the Son.

REFERENCES

Gen. 1:1–2; Matt. 4:1; 28:19; John 14:16; 15:26; Acts 5:3–4; 9:31; 1 Cor. 3:16; 6:19; 2 Cor. 1:21–22; Gal. 4:6; Eph. 1:13; 3:14; 1 Pet. 1:2; 4:14.

SCRIPTURE: JOHN 15:26

"But when the Helper comes, whom I will send to you from the Father, the Spirit of truth, who proceeds from the Father, he will bear witness about me."

What roles does the Holy Spirit fulfill in Christians?

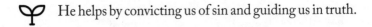 He helps by convicting us of sin and guiding us in truth.

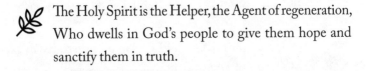 The Holy Spirit is the Helper, the Agent of regeneration, Who dwells in God's people to give them hope and sanctify them in truth.

The Holy Spirit is the Helper promised by Jesus Christ, the Agent of regeneration, Who dwells in God's people to unite them with the Father and the Son, give them hope of salvation, and sanctify them in God's truth.

REFERENCES

John 14:26; 16:7–11, 13–15, 17:17; Acts 1:8; 2:4–11; 4:31; 16:6–10; Rom. 8:10–11, 26–27; 1 Cor. 2:10–11; 3:16; 12:7–11; Gal. 5:16–25; Eph. 1:13, 17–20.

SCRIPTURE: GALATIANS 5:22–23

"But the fruit of the Spirit is love, joy, peace, patience, kindness, goodness, faithfulness, gentleness, self-control; against such things there is no law."

What roles does the Holy Spirit fulfill in the church?

 He is the Author of Scripture and the Unifier of God's people.

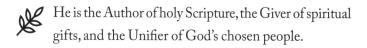 He is the Author of holy Scripture, the Giver of spiritual gifts, and the Unifier of God's chosen people.

He is the Agent of divinely inspired Scripture Who guided the prophets and Apostles into truth as they wrote the Holy Bible. He gives spiritual gifts to each member of the Church and is the Source of unity and communion among God's chosen people.

REFERENCES

John 14:26; 16:7–11, 13–15; Acts 1:8; 2: 4–11; 4:31; Rom. 8:10–11, 26–27; 1 Cor. 2:10–11; 3:16; 12:7–11; Gal. 5:16–25; Eph. 1:13, 17–20; 5:18–21; 2 Peter 1:21.

SCRIPTURE: 1 CORINTHIANS 12:7

"To each is given the manifestation of the Spirit for the common good."

What roles does the Holy Spirit fulfill in the world?

 He convicts humanity of sin, righteousness, and judgment.

 The Holy Spirit carries out the Father's will for the world, and convicts humanity of sin, righteousness, and judgment.

 The Holy Spirit carries out the Father's will for the world and the Church and convicts humanity of sin, righteousness, and of the judgment to come.

REFERENCES

John 15:26; 16:8–11.

SCRIPTURE: JOHN 16:8-11

"And when he comes, he will convict the world concerning sin and righteousness and judgment: concerning sin, because they do not believe in me; concerning righteousness, because I go to the Father, and you will see me no longer; concerning judgment, because the ruler of this world is judged."

Parents, sit down with your child and joyfully examine their memorization of questions 21-40.

The aim is substantial memorization, not perfect memorization. Remember, there is no timeline for this exam to be completed. It may take one try or several. The goal is consistent and faithful mental discipleship until your child can recite and understand these questions and answers within their category (seedlings, sprouts, or vines).

Do not move on until your child has completed this Block exam. Once the exam is completed, your child no longer has to practice or recite the content within this Block and can move onto the memorization of the following Block.

MAN

Block 03 • Questions 41–55

What is a human being?

 A creature of God made in the image of God.

 A human being is a living creature of God made in the image and likeness of God.

 A human being is a living creature of God made in the image and likeness of God.

REFERENCES

Gen 1:26–27; 2:7; Psalm 8:4; 139:14.

SCRIPTURE: GENESIS 1:26

"Then God said, "Let us make man in our image, after our likeness. And let them have dominion over the fish of the sea and over the birds of the heavens and over the livestock and over all the earth and over every creeping thing that creeps on the earth.""

Who were the first human beings?

 The first human beings were Adam and Eve.

 The first human being was Adam, who was formed from the dust, and His wife Eve, who was made from Adam's rib.

 The first human being was Adam, who was formed by God from the dust of the ground, and His wife Eve, who was made from Adam's rib.

REFERENCES
Gen. 1:26–27; 2:5–8, 18–23; 4:1, 25; 5:1–5; 1 Cor. 15:45; 1 Tim. 2:13.

SCRIPTURE: GENESIS 2:18
"Then the Lord God said, "It is not good that the man should be alone; I will make him a helper fit for him.""

How many genders do human beings have?

 There are only two genders: Male and female.

 Human beings have only two genders. Male is the gender for men and boys, and female is the gender for women and girls.

 Human beings have only two genders. Male is the gender for men and boys, and female is the gender for women and girls. God assigns each person their permanent gender according to His perfect will.

REFERENCES

Gen. 1:27; 5:2; 6:19; 7:2–16 (gender in animals, too); Matt. 19:4; Mark 10:6; Gal. 3:28.

SCRIPTURE: GENESIS 1:27

"So God created man in his own image, in the image of God he created him; male and female he created them."

QUESTION 44
Why did God make man and woman?

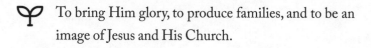 To bring Him glory, to produce families, and to be an image of Jesus and His Church.

God made man and woman to bring Him glory, for the purpose of marriage and children, and to be an image of Christ and His Church.

God made man and woman to bring Him glory, for the purpose of marriage, for the ability to produce children, and to be a physical reflection of the coming marriage between Christ and His church.

REFERENCES
Ps. 16:5–11; 19:1; 86:9; 144:15; Isa. 12:2; 60:21; Jer. 9:23, 24; Luke 2:10; Rom. 11:36; 1 Cor. 6:20; 10:31; Phil. 4:4; Rev. 4:11; 21:3–4.

SCRIPTURE: 1 CORINTHIANS 11:7
"For a man ought not to cover his head, since he is the image and glory of God, but woman is the glory of man."

78

How were human beings given life?

 God breathed life into Adam, giving him physical and spiritual life.

 God breathed the breath of life into the nostrils of Adam, giving him physical and spiritual life.

 God breathed the breath of life into the nostrils of Adam, giving him and all that came from him physical and spiritual life.

REFERENCES

Gen. 1:1, 26–28; 2:7, 21–23; Ps. 8; Eph 4:24; Col. 3:10.

SCRIPTURE: GENESIS 2:7

"Then the Lord God formed the man of dust from the ground and breathed into his nostrils the breath of life, and the man became a living creature."

What did God give Adam and Eve besides their bodies?

 God gave Adam and Eve living and eternal souls.

 God gave Adam and Eve eternal souls that remain spiritually alive only when they are united to God.

 God gave Adam and Eve eternal souls designed to know and worship Him; the soul remains spiritually alive only when it is united to God.

REFERENCES
Gen. 2:7; Deut. 4:29; 6:5; 10:12; 11:13, 18; 13:3; Ecc. 12:7; Ezek. 18:4; Matt. 10:28; 16:26; 22:37; 3 John 1:2.

SCRIPTURE: EZEKIEL 18:4
"Behold, all souls are mine; the soul of the father as well as the soul of the son is mine: the soul who sins shall die."

What command and warning did God give to Adam?

 To not eat from the forbidden tree or he would die.

 God commanded Adam not to eat from the Forbidden Tree, and if he did, he would surely die.

 God commanded Adam to eat of every tree in the Garden of Eden except the Tree of the Knowledge of Good and Evil, and if he did, he would surely die.

REFERENCES

Gen. 2:16–17; 3:17; Hos. 6:7; Rom. 5:14; 1 Cor. 15:22.

SCRIPTURE: GENESIS 2:16–17

"And the Lord God commanded the man, saying, "You may surely eat of every tree of the garden, but of the tree of the knowledge of good and evil you shall not eat, for in the day that you eat of it you shall surely die.'"

What does it mean to die?

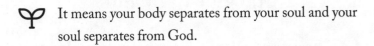 It means your body separates from your soul and your soul separates from God.

It means your body separates from your soul, which is physical death, or your soul separates from God, which is spiritual death.

It means your body separates from your soul, which is physical death, or your soul separates from God, which is spiritual death.

REFERENCES
Gen. 2:17; 3:8; 5:5; 6:17; Matt. 27:50; Rom. 5:12; 6:23; Heb. 2:9; 9:27; Rev. 21:4.

SCRIPTURE: ROMANS 5:12
"Therefore, just as sin came into the world through one man, and death through sin, and so death spread to all men because all sinned…"

QUESTION 49
Did Adam obey God's command?

 No. The serpent tempted Eve, and she and Adam both ate, disobeying God.

 No. The serpent tempted Eve to eat of the forbidden tree, and she and Adam both ate, disobeying God.

 No. The serpent tempted Eve to eat the fruit of the forbidden tree, she ate and offered the fruit to Adam, and He ate, disobeying God.

REFERENCES
Gen. 3:6, 16–19; Rom. 5:14.

SCRIPTURE: GENESIS 3:17
"And to Adam he said, 'Because you have listened to the voice of your wife and have eaten of the tree of which I commanded you, 'You shall not eat of it, cursed is the ground because of you; in pain you shall eat of it all the days of your life...'"

83

Did Adam and Eve die as God promised?

 Yes. Their bodies began to die, and their souls lost their life as God separated them from Himself.

 Yes. Because of their sin, their bodies began to die, and their souls lost their spiritual life as God separated them from Himself.

 Yes. Because of their sin, their bodies began to die, and their souls lost their spiritual life as they were separated from God by His removal of them from His presence in the Garden.

REFERENCES

Gen. 3:8; 5:5; Rom. 5:14; 1 Cor. 15:22; Eph. 4:18.

SCRIPTURE: GENESIS 5:5

"Thus all the days that Adam lived were 930 years, and he died."

Is this why all human beings die?

 Yes, Adam's sinful nature has been passed down to all people. We are born sinners, separated from God, and have bodies that die.

 Yes. Like a disease, Adam's sinful nature has been passed down to all his descendants. Therefore, all humans are born in sin, with souls separated from God and bodies that decay from conception.

 Yes. Like a spiritual disease, Adam's sinful nature has been passed down to all his descendants. Therefore, all humans are born with original sin having souls separated from the spiritual life of God, and have physical bodies that decay from the point of conception.

REFERENCES
Gen. 2:16-17; 3:16–19, 23; Rom. 3:16; 5:12–21; 1 Cor. 15–22; Eph. 2:1; Jas. 2:10.

SCRIPTURE: ROMANS 6:23
"For the wages of sin is death, but the free gift of God is eternal life in Christ Jesus our Lord."

What would have happened if Adam and Eve never sinned?

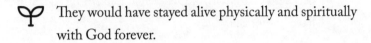 They would have stayed alive physically and spiritually with God forever.

If Adam and Eve would have never sinned, they would have stayed alive physically and spiritually in the presence of God forever.

If Adam and Eve would have never sinned, they would have remained alive physically and spiritually in a perfect world, in the presence of God, forever.

REFERENCES
Gen. 2:15–17, 24–25; Heb. 7:11; Rev. 21:1–4.

SCRIPTURE: GENESIS 2:25
"And the man and his wife were both naked and were not ashamed."

After they sinned, What was Adam and Eve's greatest need?

 A Redeemer to pay for their sin, resurrect them spiritually, and reconcile them to God.

 Adam and Eve's greatest need was for a Redeemer to atone for their sin, resurrect their spiritually dead souls, reconcile them back to God, and give them eternal life.

 Adam and Eve's greatest need was for a Redeemer to atone for their sin, resurrect their spiritually dead souls, reconcile them back to God, and give them eternal life.

REFERENCES

Gen. 3:15, 21, 24; Isa. 59:2; John 3:3; Rom. 5:8; 6:23; 2 Cor. 5:17; 1 John 1:9.

SCRIPTURE: GENESIS 3:14-15

The Lord God said to the serpent... I will put enmity between you and the woman, and between your offspring and her offspring; he shall bruise your head, and you shall bruise his heel.

How is a person's soul resurrected from spiritual death?

 By being born again of the Spirit of God.

 A person's soul is resurrected by being born again of the Spirit of God. We cannot spiritually birth ourselves; it is a sovereign work of God wherein a person is given new spiritual life, repentance, and the gift of faith.

 A person's soul is resurrected through being born again of the Spirit of God. Just as humans cannot physically birth themselves, they cannot initiate this new spiritual life on their own; it requires a supernatural and sovereign work of God. This spiritual resurrection reunites a person with God, reconnecting them to the source of spiritual life and granting them a heart of repentance and the gift of faith.

REFERENCES

Deut. 30:6; Isa. 45:22; Ezek. 36:26–27; Matt 11:28–30; John 3:3–5, 8; 6:44–45; 15:5; Acts 16:14; 26:18; Rom. 10:17; 1 Cor. 1:9; 2:10, 12–16; 4:6; Eph. 1:17–18, 2:8-9; 3:17; Phil. 1:29; Titus 3:4–7; 1 John 5:1; Rev. 22:17.

"Jesus answered him, "Truly, truly, I say to you, unless one is born again he cannot see the kingdom of God."

JOHN 3:3

Did Jesus need a
spiritual resurrection?

 No. Jesus was not born of Adam but of God. He was spiritually alive from birth and lived without sin.

 No. Jesus was not conceived of Adam but of the Spirit of God. Therefore, He wasn't born spiritually dead but spiritually alive and without sin, making Him a worthy sacrifice for the sins of His people.

 No. Jesus was not conceived of the seed of Adam but of the Spirit of God. Therefore, He wasn't born spiritually dead but spiritually alive and without original sin, making Him a worthy sacrifice for the sins of His people.

REFERENCES
Isa. 53:9; Matt. 1:18, 28:18; John 1:1–5, 14; 10:30; 2 Cor. 5:21; Titus 2:11–13; Heb. 4:15; 9:14.

SCRIPTURE: MATTHEW 1:18
"When his mother Mary had been betrothed to Joseph, before they came together she was found to be with child from the Holy Spirit."

BLOCK #3 MAN: VERBAL EXAM

Parents, sit down with your child and joyfully examine their memorization of questions 41-55.

The aim is substantial memorization, not perfect memorization. Remember, there is no timeline for this exam to be completed. It may take one try or several. The goal is consistent and faithful mental discipleship until your child can recite and understand these questions and answers within their category (seedlings, sprouts, or vines).

Do not move on until your child has completed this Block exam. Once the exam is completed, your child no longer has to practice or recite the content within this Block and can move onto the memorization of the following Block.

LAW

Block 04 • Questions 56–70

What does God require of all human beings?

 Perfect obedience to His Law.

 God requires perfect obedience to His Law from all human beings.

 God requires perfect and total obedience from the heart, mind, and body to His Moral Law from all human beings.

REFERENCES

Lev. 11:44–45; 19:2; 19:18; 20:7; Num. 15:40; Deut. 6:5; 29:29; Mic. 6:8; Matt 5:48; 22:37–39; 1 Peter 1:15–16; Jas. 2:10; 1 John 5:2–3.

SCRIPTURE: MATTHEW 5:48

"You therefore must be perfect, as your heavenly Father is perfect."

What is God's Moral Law?

 The Ten Commandments.

 God's Moral Law is His revealed will for human worship and behavior seen in the Ten Commandments recorded in Exodus 20.

 God's Moral Law is His revealed will for human worship and behavior seen in the Ten Commandments recorded in Exodus 20. The perfect keeping of these commandments leads to eternal life, and the breaking of even one of these commandments leads to eternal death.

REFERENCES
Exod. 20:1–17; Deut. 4:13; 5:6–21; Matt. 19:17–19; Jas. 2:10.

SCRIPTURE: DEUTERONOMY 4:13
"And he declared to you his covenant, which he commanded you to perform, that is, the Ten Commandments, and he wrote them on two tablets of stone."

Can any human being perfectly keep the Ten Commandments?

 No. We are all born with a desire to sin and break God's commandments.

 No. All human beings are born with a desire to sin, a hatred for God, and break God's commandments.

 No. From birth, the highest desire of the human heart is sin. This sinful state leads them to hate God, love themselves, and break God's commandments.

REFERENCES

Gen. 9:21; Ps. 1:1–2; Prov. 20:9; Ecc. 7:20; Rom. 3:9–12, 19–20, 23; 7:14–15, 22–25; 1 Cor. 13:9; Phil. 3:12–16; Jas. 2:10; 1 John 1:8.

SCRIPTURE: ROMANS 3:10

"As it is written: "None is righteous, no, not one…""

If humanity can't keep the Moral Law, why does God require that we do?

 So that we can see our great need for a Savior.

 Because our inability to keep the Ten Commandments reveals our sinfulness and teaches us about God's standard for righteousness, showing us our need for a Savior.

 Because our inability to keep the Ten Commandments reveals our sinfulness and teaches us about God's standard for righteousness, showing us our need for a Savior.

REFERENCES
Ps. 32:5; Rom. 3:19-26; 7:7, 24, 25; 1 Cor. 9:24; Phil. 3:12–14; 1 John 1:9; 3:1–3.

SCRIPTURE: ROMANS 3:19-20
"Now we know that whatever the law says it speaks to those who are under the law, so that every mouth may be stopped, and the whole world may be held accountable to God. For by works of the law no human being will be justified in his sight, since through the law comes knowledge of sin."

QUESTION 60

What is the first commandment?

 You shall have no other gods before me.

 The first commandment is: You shall have no other gods before me.

 The first commandment is: You shall have no other gods before me.

REFERENCES
Exod. 20:3; Deut. 5:7.

SCRIPTURE: MATTHEW 4:10
"Then Jesus said to him, "Be gone, Satan! For it is written, "'You shall worship the Lord your God and him only shall you serve.'"

What is the second commandment?

 You shall have no idols.

 The second command is: You shall not make for yourself a carved image. You shall not bow down to them or serve them, for I the Lord your God am a jealous God.

 The second commandment is: You shall not make for yourself a carved image, or any likeness of anything that is in heaven above, or that is in the earth beneath, or that is in the water under the earth. You shall not bow down to them or serve them, for I the Lord your God am a jealous God.

REFERENCES
Exod. 20:4-6; Deut. 5:8-10.

SCRIPTURE: EXODUS 20:4–5
"You shall not make for yourself a carved image, or any likeness of anything that is in heaven above, or that is in the earth beneath, or that is in the water under the earth. You shall not bow down to them or serve them, for I the Lord your God am a jealous God..."

What is the third commandment?

 You shall not take the Lord's name in vain.

 The third commandment is: You shall not take the name of the Lord your God in vain.

 The third commandment is: You shall not take the name of the Lord your God in vain, for the Lord will not hold him guiltless who takes His name in vain.

REFERENCES
Exod. 20:7; Deut. 5:11.

SCRIPTURE: EXODUS 20:7
"You shall not take the name of the Lord your God in vain, for the Lord will not hold him guiltless who takes his name in vain."

What is the fourth commandment?

 Keep the Sabbath day holy.

 The fourth commandment is: Remember the Sabbath day, to keep it holy. Six days you shall labor, and do all your work, but the seventh day is a Sabbath to the Lord your God. On it you shall not do any work.

 The fourth commandment is: Remember the Sabbath day, to keep it holy. Six days you shall labor, and do all your work, but the seventh day is a Sabbath to the Lord your God. On it you shall not do any work, you, or your son, or your daughter, your male servant, or your female servant, or your livestock, or the sojourner who is within your gates. For in six days the Lord made heaven and earth, the sea, and all that is in them, and rested on the seventh day.

REFERENCES
20:8-11; Deut. 5:12-15.

SCRIPTURE: EXODUS 20:8
"Remember the Sabbath day, to keep it holy."

What is the fifth commandment?

 Honor your father and your mother.

 The fifth commandment is: Honor your father and your mother that your days may be long in the land.

 The fifth commandment is: Honor your father and your mother, that your days may be long in the land that the Lord your God is giving you.

REFERENCES
Exod. 20:12; Deut. 5:16.

SCRIPTURE: EPHESIANS 6:1-4
Children, obey your parents in the Lord, for this is right. "Honor your father and mother" (this is the first commandment with a promise), "that it may go well with you and that you may live long in the land." Fathers, do not provoke your children to anger, but bring them up in the discipline and instruction of the Lord.

"Honor your father and your mother, that your
days may be long in the land that the Lord your
God is giving you."

EXODUS 20:12

What is the six commandment?

 You shall not murder.

 The sixth commandment is: You shall not murder.

 The sixth commandment is: You shall not murder.

REFERENCES
Exod. 20:13; Deut. 5:17.

SCRIPTURE: MATTHEW 5:21-22
"You have heard that it was said to those of old, 'You shall not murder; and whoever murders will be liable to judgment.' But I say to you that everyone who is angry with his brother will be liable to judgment; whoever insults his brother will be liable to the council; and whoever says, 'You fool!' will be liable to the hell of fire."

What is the seventh commandment?

 You shall not commit adultery.

 The seventh commandment is: You shall not commit adultery.

 The seventh commandment is: You shall not commit adultery.

REFERENCES
Exod. 20:14; Deut. 5:18.

SCRIPTURE: MATTHEW 5:27-28
"You have heard that it was said, 'You shall not commit adultery.' But I say to you that everyone who looks at a woman with lustful intent has already committed adultery with her in his heart."

What is the eighth commandment?

 You shall not steal.

 The eighth commandment is: You shall not steal.

 The eighth commandment is: You shall not steal.

REFERENCES

Exod. 20:15; Deut. 5:19

SCRIPTURE: EPHESIANS 4:28

"Let the thief no longer steal, but rather let him labor, doing honest work with his own hands, so that he may have something to share with anyone in need."

What is the ninth commandment?

 You shall not lie.

 The ninth commandment is: You shall not lie

 The ninth commandment is: You shall not bear false witness against your neighbor.

REFERENCES
Exod. 20:16; Deut. 5:20.

SCRIPTURE: PROVERBS 19:5
"A false witness will not go unpunished, and he who breathes out lies will not escape."

What is the tenth commandment?

 You shall not covet things that are not yours.

 The tenth commandment is: You shall not covet your neighbor's possessions.

 The tenth commandment is: You shall not covet your neighbor's house; you shall not covet your neighbor's wife, or his male servant, or his female servant, or his ox, or his donkey, or anything that is your neighbor's.

REFERENCES
Exod. 20:17; Deut. 5:21.

SCRIPTURE: 1 TIMOTHY 6:6-8
"But godliness with contentment is great gain, for we brought nothing into the world, and we cannot take anything out of the world. But if we have food and clothing, with these we will be content."

What is the summary of the Ten Commandments given to us by the Lord Jesus Christ?

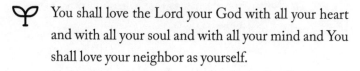

You shall love the Lord your God with all your heart and with all your soul and with all your mind and You shall love your neighbor as yourself.

The summary of the Ten Commandments is: You shall love the Lord your God with all your heart and with all your soul and with all your mind. This is the great and first commandment. And a second is like it: You shall love your neighbor as yourself.

The summary of the Ten Commandments is: You shall love the Lord your God with all your heart and with all your soul and with all your mind. This is the great and first commandment. And a second is like it: You shall love your neighbor as yourself. On these two commandments depend all the Law and the Prophets..

REFERENCES
Deut 6:4–5; Matt. 22:37–40; Mark 12:29–30.

"Hear, O Israel: The Lord our God, the Lord is one. You shall love the Lord your God with all your heart and with all your soul and with all your might. And these words that I command you today shall be on your heart. You shall teach them diligently to your children, and shall talk of them when you sit in your house, and when you walk by the way, and when you lie down, and when you rise. You shall bind them as a sign on your hand, and they shall be as frontlets between your eyes. You shall write them on the doorposts of your house and on your gates."

Parents, sit down with your child and joyfully examine their memorization of questions 56-70.

The aim is substantial memorization, not perfect memorization. Remember, there is no timeline for this exam to be completed. It may take one try or several. The goal is consistent and faithful mental discipleship until your child can recite and understand these questions and answers within their category (seedlings, sprouts, or vines).

Do not move on until your child has completed this Block exam. Once the exam is completed, your child no longer has to practice or recite the content within this Block and can move onto the memorization of the following Block.

CHURCH

Block 05 • Questions 71–86

What is the Covenant of Grace?

 An eternal agreement within the Trinity to save the elect through faith in Jesus Christ.

 The Covenant of Grace is an eternal agreement within the Trinity to save the elect through faith in Jesus Christ. While it remains the same covenant, it was administered differently under the Old Testament and New Testament.

 The Covenant of Grace is an eternal agreement within the Trinity to save the elect through faith in Jesus Christ and was administered differently in the time of the law and the gospel. Under the law, it was administered through promises, prophecies, sacrifices, circumcision, and other ordinances for the Jews, pointing to the coming Christ, known as the Old Testament. During the time of the gospel, Christ, the substance, was revealed, and the covenant is now administered through preaching, baptism, and the Lord's Supper, known as the New Testament. Therefore, there is not two Covenants of Grace but one that is administered differently in various eras

REFERENCES

Gal. 3:21; Rom. 8:3; Rom. 3:20,21; Gen. 3:15; Isa. 42:6. Mark 16:15,16; John 3:16; Rom. 10:6,9; Gal. 3:11. Heb. 9:15-17; Heb. 7:22; Luke 22:20; 1 Cor. 11:25; 2 Cor. 3:6-9; Heb. chap. 8 to 10; Rom. 4:11; Col. 2:11,12; 1 Cor. 5:7; 1 Cor. 10:1-4; Heb. 11:13; John 8:56; Gal. 3:7-9,14; Col. 2:17; Matt. 28:19,20; 1 Cor. 11:23-25; Heb. 12:22-28; Jer. 31:33,34; Eph. 2:15-19; Gal. 3:14,16; Rom 3:21-23,30; Ps. 32:1 with Rom. 4:3,6,16,17,23,24; Heb. 13:8; Acts 15:11.

SCRIPTURE: JEREMIAH 31:31-34

"Behold, the days are coming, declares the Lord, when I will make a new covenant with the house of Israel and the house of Judah, not like the covenant that I made with their fathers on the day when I took them by the hand to bring them out of the land of Egypt, my covenant that they broke, though I was their husband, declares the Lord. For this is the covenant that I will make with the house of Israel after those days, declares the Lord: I will put my law within them, and I will write it on their hearts. And I will be their God, and they shall be my people. And no longer shall each one teach his neighbor and each his brother, saying, 'Know the Lord,' for they shall all know me, from the least of them to the greatest, declares the Lord. For I will forgive their iniquity, and I will remember their sin no more."

What is the Church of Jesus Christ?

 The people of God who are saved by God's grace for God's own glory.

 The church of Jesus Christ is the people of God who were elected to salvation by God's grace for His own glory. Jesus is the head of this church and preserves it to everlasting life.

 The church of Jesus Christ is the covenant people of God who, before the foundation of the world, were elected to salvation by God's sovereign grace for His own glory. Jesus Christ is the head of this church, whereby His Spirit and His Word gathers it, defends it, unifies it, and preserves it to everlasting life.

REFERENCES

Gen. 2:4; Ps. 23:6; 129:1–5; Isa. 59:21; John 10:11; Matt. 16:18; John 10:27–30; Acts 2:42–47; 20:28; Rom. 1:16; 8:29; 10:14–17; 1 Cor. 1:4–9; 11:26; Eph. 1:3–14; 4:1–6; 11–13; 5:26; Col. 1:18. 1 Pet. 1:3–5; 1 John 3:14, 19–21; Rev. 5:9.

"There is one body and one Spirit—just as you were called to the one hope that belongs to your call— one Lord, one faith, one baptism, one God and Father of all, who is over all and through all and in all."

How does a person become a member of the church of Jesus Christ?

 By a profession of faith in Jesus and through water baptism.

 A person becomes a member of the church by a public profession of faith in Jesus Christ and through water baptism.

 A person becomes a member of the church by a public profession of faith in Jesus Christ and through water baptism.

REFERENCES
Deut. 30:6; Isa. 45:22; Ezek. 36:26–27; Matt 11:28–30; John 3:3–5; 6:44–45; 15:5; Acts 16:14; 26:18; Rom. 10:17; 1 Cor. 1:9; 2:10, 12–16; 4:6; Eph. 1:17–18; 2:8; 3:17; Phil. 1:29; Titus 3:4–7; Rev. 22:17.

SCRIPTURE: JOHN 3:5
"Jesus answered, "Truly, truly, I say to you, unless one is born of water and the Spirit, he cannot enter the kingdom of God."

What are the two church sacraments?

 Water baptism and the Lord's Supper.

 The two church sacraments are water baptism and the Lord's Supper. They are physical practices that help Christians understand the spiritual promises of the Gospel.

 The two church sacraments are water baptism and the Lord's Supper. They are visible signs and seals instituted by God to help His people remember their spiritual identity, the promises we receive in the Gospel, and the grace of God through the work of Jesus Christ.

REFERENCES
Matt. 28:19; 26:26-28; Mark 14:22-25; Luke 22:19-20; 1 Cor. 1:22-26; 10:16–17; 11:23–26; Gal. 3:27.

SCRIPTURE: LUKE 22:19-20
And he took bread, and when he had given thanks, he broke it and gave it to them, saying, "This is my body, which is given for you. Do this in remembrance of me."

What is water baptism?

 A sign and seal of the Covenant of Grace applied to the body by water.

 Water baptism is a sign and seal of the Covenant of Grace applied to the body by water. It's signifies the washing away of sin and imparts the blessings of the covenant to its recipients but it does not regenerate or save a person.

 Water baptism is a sign and seal of the Covenant of Grace applied to the body by water. It's signifies the washing away of sin and imparts the blessings of the covenant to its recipients but it does not save a person. It is the initiating rite into the visible church and is to be administered in the name of the Father, the Son, and the Holy Spirit.

REFERENCES
Matt. 28:19; Gal. 3:27; Acts 2:38–39; Mark 1:4; Acts 22:16; Rom. 6:3–5; Col. 2:11-12.

SCRIPTURE: MATTHEW 28:19
"Go therefore and make disciples of all nations, baptizing them in the name of the Father and of the Son and of the Holy Spirit."

What is the Lord's Supper?

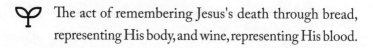

The act of remembering Jesus's death through bread, representing His body, and wine, representing His blood.

The Lord's Supper is the ongoing act of remembering and proclaiming the reconciling power of Jesus's death through bread that represents His body and wine that represents His blood. It is a sign to teach believers that, in the same way food and drink nourish our bodies, Christ's body and blood nourish our soul.

The Lord's Supper is the ongoing act of remembering and proclaiming the reconciling power of Jesus's death through bread that represents His body and wine that represents His blood. It is a sign to teach believers that, in the same way food and drink nourish our bodies, Christ's body and blood nourish our soul. Before taking this sacrament, one should engage in self-examination and heartfelt repentance through faith, committing to further obedience to the Lord.

REFERENCES
1 Cor. 10:16–17, 21; 11:23–34.

"For I received from the Lord what I also delivered to you, that the Lord Jesus on the night when he was betrayed took bread, and when he had given thanks, he broke it, and said, 'This is my body, which is for you. Do this in remembrance of me.' In the same way also he took the cup, after supper, saying, 'This cup is the new covenant in my blood. Do this, as often as you drink it, in remembrance of me.' For as often as you eat this bread and drink the cup, you proclaim the Lord's death until he comes."

Who can take the Lord's Supper?

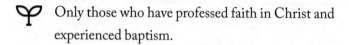 Only those who have professed faith in Christ and experienced baptism.

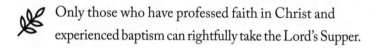 Only those who have professed faith in Christ and experienced baptism can rightfully take the Lord's Supper.

Only those who have, professed faith in Christ, experienced baptism, and can engage in self-examination and remembrance of the cross can rightfully take the Lord's Supper.

REFERENCES
Ps. 50:16; Isa. 1:11–17; 1 Cor. 10:19–22; 11:17–34.

SCRIPTURE: LUKE 22:19-20
"And he took bread, and when he had given thanks, he broke it and gave it to them, saying, "This is my body, which is given for you. Do this in remembrance of me." And likewise the cup after they had eaten, saying, "This cup that is poured out for you is the new covenant in my blood.'"

What is The Lord's Day?

 Sunday—the first day of the week and is also the Christian Sabbath.

 The Lord's Day is Sunday—the first day of the week. This is the Christian Sabbath and is to be set apart for worship and rest.

 The Lord's Day is Sunday—the first day of the week. This is the Christian Sabbath and is to be set apart for worship, ministry, and physical rest from our regular duties of common life.

REFERENCES

Exod 20:8, 10; Lev. 23:3; Neh. 13:15–22; Isa. 58:13–14; Matt. 12:1–13; Mark 2:27-28; Luke 4:16; Acts 20:7; 1 Cor. 16:2; Rev. 1:10.

SCRIPTURE: ACTS 20:7

"On the first day of the week, when we were gathered together to break bread, Paul talked with them, intending to depart on the next day, and he prolonged his speech until midnight."

What are the two offices of church government?

 Elder and Deacon.

 The two offices of church government are Elder and Deacon. Elders are qualified men who shepherd the church, and deacons are qualified men who serve the church.

 The two offices of church government are Elder and Deacon. Elders are qualified men who oversee the spiritual condition of the congregation through prayer, preaching, and administering sacraments, while deacons are qualified men who meet the physical needs through acts of service.

REFERENCES
Acts 6:3–6; 14:23; 20:17, 28; 1 Cor. 9:6–14; Gal. 6:6–7; Phil. 1:1; 1 Tim. 3:2; 4:14; 5:17–18; 2 Tim. 2:4; Heb. 13:17.

SCRIPTURE: ACTS 20:28
"Pay careful attention to yourselves and to all the flock, in which the Holy Spirit has made you overseers, to care for the church of God, which he obtained with his own blood."

What is the mission of the Church?

 To proclaim the Gospel and the reign and rule of Christ over all things.

 The mission of the church is to proclaim the reign and rule of Christ over all things. This is carried out in the Great Commission through the proclamation of the Gospel and by the discipling of the nations according to God's Word.

 The mission of the church is to proclaim the reign and rule of Christ over all things, carried out through the Great Commission. This involves proclaiming the Gospel, baptizing and discipling nations, and guiding people in all aspects of life according to God's Word.

REFERENCES
Matt. 28:16-20; Mark 13:10; 14:9; Luke 24:44-49; John 20:21; Acts 1:8.

THE GREAT COMMISSION

"And Jesus came and said to them, "All authority
in heaven and on earth has been given to me.
Go therefore and make disciples of all nations,
baptizing them in the name of the Father and of
the Son and of the Holy Spirit, teaching them
to observe all that I have commanded you. And
behold, I am with you always, to the end of the age."

MATTHEW 28:18–20

Will the church be successful in carrying out the Great Commission?

 Yes, the gates of hell will not prevail against the church.

 Yes, the church will be successful because Christ is the head of the church. He is a victorious King who has promised to build His church and that the gates of hell will not prevail against it.

 Yes, the church will be successful because Christ is the head of the church. He is a victorious King with all authority in heaven and on earth and has promised to build His church through the preaching of the Gospel, and the gates of hell will not prevail against it.

REFERENCES
Matt. 16:18; 28:16-20; Mark 13:10; 14:9; Luke 24:44-49; John 20:21; Acts 1:8; Eph. 5:23.

SCRIPTURE: MATTHEW 16:18
"And I tell you, you are Peter, and on this rock I will build my church, and the gates of hell shall not prevail against it."

What is the Kingdom of God?

 The collective community and influence of those who submit to Christ as King.

 The Kingdom of God is the collective community and influence of those who submit to Christ as King. This Kingdom was started by Jesus's ministry and ascension, it advances always, and is completed at Christ's final return.

 The Kingdom of God is the collective community and influence of those who submit to Christ as King. This Kingdom was inaugurated at the ministry and ascension of Jesus to the Father, it increases and advances progressively, and will be fully consummated at Christ's final return.

REFERENCES
1 Chron. 29:11; Matt. 3:2; 4:17, 23; 5:3, 10, 19–20; 6:10, 33; 13:11–41; 28:18 Luke 10:11; 11:20; John 18:36; Acts 1:6–8; Phil. 3:20.

SCRIPTURE: MATTHEW 6:9-10
"Our Father in heaven, hallowed be your name. Your kingdom come, your will be done, on earth as it is in heaven."

How will the Kingdom of God grow?

 By God's people proclaiming the Gospel, representing Jesus, and establishing the rule of Christ in all areas of life.

 The Kingdom of God will grow by the power of Christ through the faithfulness of the saints. Namely, through Gospel proclamation, Christian representation, and establishing the rule of Christ in all areas of life.

 The Kingdom of God will grow by the power of Christ through the faithful submission of the saints to His reign and rule over their lives. Namely, His people will proclaim the Gospel, represent their King in their community, and establish the righteous rule of Christ in all areas of life.

REFERENCES

Matt. 13:33; Mark 4:1–9, 13–20, 26–29, 30–32; 1 Cor. 1:26–29; 3:5–7; Acts 1:8; Eph. 4:15–16.

SCRIPTURE: MATTHEW 13:33

"But you will receive power when the Holy Spirit has come upon you, and you will be my witnesses in Jerusalem and in all Judea and Samaria, and to the end of the earth."

Will the Kingdom of God ever be defeated?

 No, because the death and resurrection of Christ is more powerful than the Fall of Adam.

 No, the Kingdom of God cannot be defeated; Christ's death and resurrection are more powerful than Adam's Fall. Jesus is victorious, He's reversing the effects of the Fall, and will not fail to redeem His people and creation.

 No, the Kingdom of God cannot be defeated; Christ's death and resurrection are more powerful than Adam's Fall. Jesus is victorious, He's reversing the effects of the Fall, and will not fail to redeem His people and creation.

REFERENCES
Matt. 16:18; 28:16-20; Mark 13:10; 14:9; Luke 24:44-49; John 20:21; Acts 1:8; Eph. 5:23.

SCRIPTURE: MATTHEW 13:33
"The kingdom of heaven is like leaven that a woman took and hid in three measures of flour, till it was all leavened."

Should Christians be optimistic about the future of the church?

 Yes, Jesus is building the church, converting sinners into saints, and bringing greater light to the world.

 Yes, Jesus is building the church, converting sinners into saints, and bringing greater light to the world.

 Yes, Jesus is building the church, converting sinners into saints, and bringing greater light to the world. This gives me great confidence that the church, through the proclamation of the Gospel and by the power of the Holy Spirit, will continue to be victorious until Christ's return.

REFERENCES
Dan. 2:44; Matt. 5:13–16; 16:18; Rom. 8:31–39; 15:13; 1 Cor. 15:50–57; Heb. 12:28; 1 John 5:4; Rev. 6:2; 17:14.

SCRIPTURE: PSALM 2:7-8
"I will tell of the decree: The Lord said to me, "You are my Son; today I have begotten you. Ask of me, and I will make the nations your heritage, and the ends of the earth your possession."

When and how will Christ return?

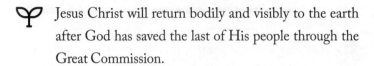

Jesus Christ will return bodily and visibly to the earth after God has saved the last of His people through the Great Commission.

As promised, Jesus Christ will return after God has saved the last of His people through the Great Commission. His return will be bodily and visibly to the earth; the dead will be raised; and Christ will judge all men in righteousness. The unrighteous will be sent to Hell and the righteous, in their resurrected bodies, will dwell on the new earth with their Lord forever.

According to His promise, Jesus Christ will return after God has saved the last of His people through the Great Commission. His return will be bodily and visibly to the earth; the dead will be raised; and Christ will judge all men in righteousness. The unrighteous will be sent to Hell, the place of everlasting punishment and spiritual death. The righteous in their resurrected and glorified bodies will receive their reward and will dwell in the glory of the new Heavens and Earth with their Lord forever.

REFERENCES

Matt. 16:27, 28:16–20; Mark 13:33; John 14:3; Acts 1:11; 17:31;
1 Cor. 15:51-52; 1 Thess. 4:16-18; Heb. 9:28; Jas. 5:7; Rev. 21:1–4.

SCRIPTURE: 1 THESSALONIANS 4:16-18

"For the Lord himself will descend from heaven with a cry of command, with the voice of an archangel, and with the sound of the trumpet of God. And the dead in Christ will rise first. Then we who are alive, who are left, will be caught up together with them in the clouds to meet the Lord in the air, and so we will always be with the Lord. Therefore encourage one another with these words."

Parents, sit down with your child and joyfully examine their memorization of questions 71-86.

The aim is substantial memorization, not perfect memorization. Remember, there is no timeline for this exam to be completed. It may take one try or several. The goal is consistent and faithful mental discipleship until your child can recite and understand these questions and answers within their category (seedlings, sprouts, or vines).

Do not move on until your child has completed this Block exam. Once the exam is completed, your child no longer has to practice or recite the content within this Block and can move onto the memorization of the following Block.

WORSHIP

Block 06 • Questions 87–91

What is Christian worship?

 Drawing near to God in spirit and in truth.

 Christian Worship is drawing near to God in spirit and in truth that He might be magnified and glorified according to His word.

 Christian Worship is drawing near to God in spirit and in truth that He might be magnified and glorified according to His word. It involves a longing for God, an enjoyment of God, and experiencing true contentment by pleasing Him through acts of obedience, praise, prayer, and service.

REFERENCES

John 4:23-24; Psalm 95:6; Romans 12:1-2; Isaiah 25:1; Hebrews 13:15; Job 1:20-21; Colossians 3:16; Psalm 29:2.

SCRIPTURE: JOHN 4:24

"God is spirit, and those who worship him must worship in spirit and truth."

How must worship be conducted?

 According to God's Word, with reverence, decently and in order.

 Worship must be conducted according to God's Word, with reverence and adoration, decently and in order. It should be directed from the heart to God the Father, through the Son, and by the Holy Spirit.

 Worship must be conducted according to God's Word, with reverence and adoration, decently and in order. It should be directed from the heart to God the Father, through the Son, and by the Holy Spirit.

REFERENCES
John 4:23–24; Eph. 2:18; 1 Cor. 14:26–40; Heb. 12:28–29.

SCRIPTURE: 1 CORINTHIANS 14:40
"But all things should be done decently and in order."

What is praise?

 It is my spiritual response to God's love through singing.

 It is my spiritual response to God's love, whereby I sing the truths of Scripture back to Him.

 Praise is worship performed through song, whereby we ascribe worth to God by singing the truths of Scripture and expressing gratitude for His love in Christ.

REFERENCES
2 Samuel 22:50; 2 Chron. 5:13; Psalm 148; 150; Rom. 15:9–11; Eph. 1:6, 12, 14; 5:18–21; Col. 3:16–17; Heb. 13:15.

SCRIPTURE: COLOSSIANS 3:16
"Let the word of Christ dwell in you richly, teaching and admonishing one another in all wisdom, singing psalms and hymns and spiritual songs, with thankfulness in your hearts to God."

What is prayer?

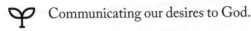 Communicating our desires to God.

 Prayer is communicating our desires to God. It's an act of worship whereby we submit ourselves to the will of God, in the name of Christ, by the help of the Holy Spirit.

 Prayer is communicating our desires to God. It's an act of worship whereby we submit ourselves to the will of God, in the name of Christ, by the help of the Holy Spirit, that we may offer thanksgiving, confession of sin, and make requests for both our own needs and the needs of others.

REFERENCES

2 Sam. 7:29; 12:21–23; Ps. 95:1–7; 65:2; John 14:13–14; Rom. 8:26; 1 Cor. 14:16–17; Phil. 4:6; 1 Tim. 2:1–2; 1 John 5:14, 16.

SCRIPTURE: PHILIPPIANS 4:6

"Do not be anxious about anything, but in everything by prayer and supplication with thanksgiving let your requests be made known to God."

"Do not be anxious about anything, but in every-thing by prayer and supplication with thanksgiving let your requests be made known to God."

PHILIPPIANS 4:6

QUESTION 91

What is preaching?

The written Word of God being proclaimed by the
mouth of man.

Preaching is the written Word of God being proclaimed
by the mouth of man. It exalts Christ, edifies the church,
and informs people of the Gospel.

Preaching is the written Word of God being proclaimed
by the mouth of man. It exalts Christ, edifies the church,
and informs people of the Gospel.

REFERENCES

*Isaiah 52:7; Matt. 4:17; 11:1; Mark 1:38; Luke 4:43; Acts
3:6; 6:4; 10:42; Rom. 1:15; 1 Cor. 1:17–23; 2 Tim. 4:1–4.*

SCRIPTURE: 2 TIMOTHY 4:1–2

"I charge you in the presence of God and of Christ
Jesus, who is to judge the living and the dead, and by his
appearing and his kingdom: preach the word; be ready
in season and out of season; reprove, rebuke, and exhort,
with complete patience and teaching."

What are spiritual gifts?

 Unique empowerments given by the Father to equip saints for effective ministry.

 Spiritual gifts are unique empowerments given by the Father for the equipping of the saints for effective ministry, building up the church, and glorifying God.

 Spiritual gifts are unique empowerments given by the Father and delivered by the Holy Spirit for the equipping of the saints for effective ministry and Christian life. When spiritual gifts are exercised rightly, they will build the church, further the Gospel, and bring glory to God.

REFERENCES

Rom. 12:3–8; 1 Cor. 12-14; Gal. 3:5; Eph. 4:11-14; 1 Thess. 5:19–22; 1 Tim. 1:18; 2 Tim. 1:6; Heb. 2:3–4; Jas. 5:13–18.

SCRIPTURE: 1 CORINTHIANS 12:4-7

"Now there are varieties of gifts, but the same Spirit; and there are varieties of service, but the same Lord; and there are varieties of activities, but it is the same God who empowers them all in everyone."

Do you have a spiritual gift?

 Yes, and it should be used to strengthen the church.

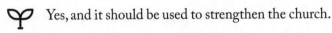 Yes, I have a spiritual gift. My spiritual gift will be aligned with Scripture, recognized by other Christians, and should be employed to strengthen the church.

 Yes, I have a spiritual gift. My spiritual gift will be aligned with Scripture, recognized by other Christians, and should be employed to strengthen the church. It may be the gift of preaching, teaching, faith, wisdom, knowledge, discernment, mercy, exhortation, giving, administration, or helps.

REFERENCES

Rom. 12:3–8; 1 Cor. 12-14; Gal. 3:5; Eph. 4:11-14; 1 Thess. 5:19–22; 1 Tim. 1:18; 2 Tim. 1:6; Heb. 2:3–4; Jas. 5:13–18.

SCRIPTURE: 1 PETER 4:10-11

"As each has received a gift, use it to serve one another, as good stewards of God's varied grace: whoever speaks, as one who speaks oracles of God; whoever serves, as one who serves by the strength that God supplies—in order that in everything God may be glorified through Jesus Christ."

What is your reasonable Christian service?

 To live a holy life that glorifies God and shows love toward others.

 My reasonable Christian service is to live a holy and sacrificial life that glorifies God and shows love toward others. My service should be motivated by God's grace toward me in Christ, and my focus is to serve God's Kingdom.

 My reasonable Christian service is to live a holy and sacrificial life that glorifies God and shows love toward others. My service should be motivated by God's grace toward me in Christ, and my focus is to serve God's Kingdom.

REFERENCES
Psalm 100:2; Mark 12:31; Rom. 12:1–2; 13:9; 1 Cor. 10:31; Gal. 5:14, 22–24; 1 Pet. 1:15–16.

SCRIPTURE: ROMANS 12:1
"I appeal to you therefore, brothers, by the mercies of God, to present your bodies as a living sacrifice, holy and acceptable to God, which is your spiritual worship."

Why should you be thankful?

 Because I am a sinner and yet God has allowed me to hear, know, and be saved by the Gospel of Jesus Christ.

 I should be thankful because I am a sinner deserving of wrath and death and yet God has allowed me to hear, know, and be saved by the Gospel of Jesus Christ. For this reason, I can rejoice in all things.

 I should be thankful because I am a sinner deserving of wrath and death and yet God has allowed me to hear, know, and be saved by the Gospel of Jesus Christ. For this reason, I can rejoice in all things.

REFERENCES
Ps. 50:23; 118; 136; Luke 22:19; 1 Cor. 1:4; 15:57; 2 Cor. 9:15; Eph. 5:18–21; Col. 3:17; 1 Thess. 5:18; Heb. 12:28; Rev. 11:17.

SCRIPTURE: COLOSSIANS 3:17
"And whatever you do, in word or deed, do everything in the name of the Lord Jesus, giving thanks to God the Father through him."

QUESTION 96

Why should you be obedient to God's Word?

 Because it glorifies God and benefits me.

 I should be obedient to God's Word because it glorifies God and benefits me. My obedience does not secure my salvation, nor does it make God love me any more.

 I should be obedient to God's Word because it glorifies God and benefits me. My obedience does not secure my salvation, nor does it make God love me any more. My only motive is His grace, and my only hope is to please Him.

REFERENCES
1:5; 6:16; 15:18; 16:26; 2 Cor. 10:5–6; 1 Pet. 1:2, 22.

SCRIPTURE: 1 JOHN 5:3
"For this is the love of God, that we keep his commandments. And his commandments are not burdensome."

BLOCK #6 WORSHIP: VERBAL EXAM

Parents, sit down with your child and joyfully examine their memorization of questions 87-96.

The aim is substantial memorization, not perfect memorization. Remember, there is no timeline for this exam to be completed. It may take one try or several. The goal is consistent and faithful mental discipleship until your child can recite and understand these questions and answers within their category (seedlings, sprouts, or vines).

Do not move on until your child has completed this Block exam. Once the exam is completed, your child no longer has to practice or recite the content within this Block and can move onto the memorization of the following Block.

MINISTRY

Block 07 • Questions 97–100

QUESTION 97

What is evangelism?

 The act of proclaiming the Gospel to others.

 Evangelism is the act of proclaiming the Gospel to others and is the responsibility of every Christian.

 Evangelism is the act of proclaiming the Gospel to others. It is the responsibility of every Christian and should be done accurately, passionately, and with clarity.

REFERENCES

Isa. 40:9–11; 52:7–10; 61:1–2; Matt. 4:17; 9:35–38; 10:32–33; 28:18–20; Mark 1:14–15; Acts 1:8; 16:25–34; Rom. 10:15; 1 Cor. 11:26; 15:1–4; 2 Cor. 2:17; 2 Tim. 1:8.

SCRIPTURE: ROMANS 10:14-15

"How then will they call on him in whom they have not believed? And how are they to believe in him of whom they have never heard? And how are they to hear without someone preaching? And how are they to preach unless they are sent? As it is written, "How beautiful are the feet of those who preach the good news!"

What should you say when you tell people the Gospel?

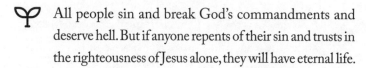 All people sin and break God's commandments and deserve hell. But if anyone repents of their sin and trusts in the righteousness of Jesus alone, they will have eternal life.

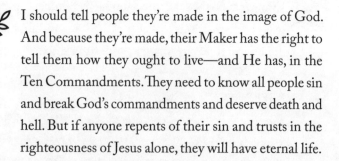 I should tell people they're made in the image of God. And because they're made, their Maker has the right to tell them how they ought to live—and He has, in the Ten Commandments. They need to know all people sin and break God's commandments and deserve death and hell. But if anyone repents of their sin and trusts in the righteousness of Jesus alone, they will have eternal life.

I should tell people they're made in the image of God. And because they're made, their Maker has the right to tell them how they ought to live—and He has, in the Ten Commandments. I should tell them all people sin and break God's commandments, and for that, they are unrighteous and deserve death and hell. However, God sent His Son Jesus to die as a substitute, to take on the wrath of God for sin, and to give His righteousness to all who would repent and trust in Him alone.

REFERENCES

Ps. 47:8; Matt. 5:48; Rom. 3:20; 5:12; 3:23; 6:23; Ezek. 18:20; Matt. 10:28; John 3:16; 10:11, 17; 1 Cor. 15:1–4, 20; John 11:25; Luke 13:3; Eph. 2:8–9; 1 Pet. 2:7.

SCRIPTURE: 1 CORINTHIANS 15:1-4

"Now I would remind you, brothers, of the gospel I preached to you, which you received, in which you stand, and by which you are being saved, if you hold fast to the word I preached to you—unless you believed in vain. For I delivered to you as of first importance what I also received: that Christ died for our sins in accordance with the Scriptures, that he was buried, that he was raised on the third day in accordance with the Scriptures."

What is the Dominion Mandate?

 God's command to mankind to be fruitful and multiply and fill the earth and subdue it and have dominion over all living creatures.

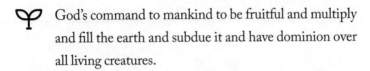 The Dominion Mandate refers to God's command to mankind to be fruitful and multiply and fill the earth and subdue it and have dominion over all living creatures. This responsibility calls Christians to reproduce God's image and exemplify His righteous rule in every sphere of life.

 The Dominion Mandate refers to God's command to mankind to be fruitful and multiply and fill the earth and subdue it and have dominion over all living creatures. This responsibility calls Christians to reproduce God's image through procreation, raise their children in the nurture and admonition of the Lord, and exemplify His righteous rule in every sphere of life.

REFERENCES

Gen. 1:26–28; 9:1, 7; 17:6, 20; 28:3; 35:11; 47:27; Exod. 1:7; Lev. 26:9; Ps. 105:24; 127:3–5; 128:3; 145:13; Jer. 23:3; Ezek. 36:11; Dan. 4:3; Mic. 4:8; Rev. 1:6.

SCRIPTURE: GENESIS 1:28

"And God blessed them. And God said to them, "Be fruitful and multiply and fill the earth and subdue it, and have dominion over the fish of the sea and over the birds of the heavens and over every living thing that moves on the earth."

What is the sum of the Christian life?

To love the Lord your God with all your heart, with all your soul, and with all your mind and to love your neighbor as yourself.

REFERENCES

Deut. 6:5; 11:1, 13; 13:3; 30:6; Josh. 22:5; Matt. 22:37–40; Mark 12:28–31; Luke 10:27.

SCRIPTURE: MARK 12:28–31

"And one of the scribes came up and heard them disputing with one another, and seeing that he answered them well, asked him, "Which commandment is the most important of all?" Jesus answered, "The most important is, 'Hear, O Israel: The Lord our God, the Lord is one. And you shall love the Lord your God with all your heart and with all your soul and with all your mind and with all your strength.' The second is this: 'You shall love your neighbor as yourself.' There is no other commandment greater than these."

FINAL VERBAL EXAM

Parents, if your child is interested in testing their ability to recite the entire 100-question catechism (within their category), give them as many opportunities as it takes to accomplish this goal.

If your child passes the verbal exam with a 90% or greater, award them with a Certificate of Completion that you can download at Relearn.org/Certificate. Print the certificate, sign it, and consider framing it. This is, even at the Seedling level, a significant intellectual and theological feat and it is worth genuine celebration.

TOPICAL INDEX

This index provides a convenient guide to help you locate specific theological topics within the catechism's questions, allowing you to explore and deepen your understanding of subjects such as God, sin, church, and more.

BAPTISM

Questions: 73, 74, 75, 77

CHURCH

Questions: 72, 73, 74, 79, 80, 81, 85

COVENANT

Questions: 71, 72, 75

THE CROSS

Questions: 15, 18

ESCHATOLOGY

Questions: 35, 36, 37, 81, 82, 85, 86

FAITH

Questions: 2, 17, 18, 19, 73, 77

GENDER

Questions: 27, 43, 44

GOD THE FATHER

Questions: 1, 3, 5, 10, 18, 19, 21, 23, 24, 25, 26

GOSPEL

Questions: 14, 19, 22, 80, 83, 95, 97, 98

HELL

Questions: 8, 20, 81, 98

JESUS CHRIST

Questions: 1, 2, 13, 14, 15, 17, 19, 20, 32, 33, 34, 35, 36, 70, 71, 72, 73, 86.

JUSTICE

Questions: 9, 11, 16,

KINGDOM

Questions: 82, 83, 84

LAW

Questions: 3, 8, 15, 56, 57, 59, 70

THE LORD'S SUPPER
Questions: 74, 76, 77

MAN
Questions: 7, 41, 42, 43, 44, 45, 46, 47, 48, 49, 50, 51, 52, 53, 54, 55

SCRIPTURE
Questions: 14, 21, 22

SIN
Questions: 6, 8, 9, 12, 16, 17, 33, 51, 58, 75, 98

THE FALL
Questions: 5, 6, 47, 49, 84,

THE HOLY SPIRIT
Questions: 19, 20, 25, 37, 38, 39, 40, 54, 55, 90, 92

TRINITY
Questions: 25, 26, 71,

WORSHIP
Questions: 78, 87, 88, 90

ACKNOWLEDGMENTS

In expressing gratitude for the completion of this book, I wanted to extend my heartfelt acknowledgments to the individuals and entities who have contributed their unwavering support and insights. Their dedication and guidance played an indispensable role in bringing this project to fruition.

1. The historical creeds and confessions, particularly the Heidelberg Catechism and the Westminster Shorter Catechism, have been instrumental in the development of this catechism. I am deeply grateful to the saints who compiled these resources.

2. Laramie Minga, the Theological Editor, for carefully reviewing and editing the manuscript to ensure doctrinal integrity and clarity.

3. Trevor West and Brittney Duron for their faithful review and insightful discussions about the manuscript, its format, and its

overall direction.

4. Jess Hall for reading, editing, and contributing to the refinement of this catechism.

5. Adam Grason for the beautiful cover design and illustrations that enhance the visual appeal of the book.

6. My four children, Aria, Honor, Valor, and Deacon who acted as the testing ground for these questions and responses.

ABOUT DALE PARTRIDGE

Dale Partridge is the Founder and President of Relearn.org and Lead Pastor at King's Way Bible Church in Prescott, Arizona.

He holds a Graduate Certificate from Western Seminary and is the author of several Christian books, including "The Manliness of Christ," "The Ground of Good Theology," and the bestselling children's book "Jesus and My Gender." You can hear his teachings on his regular podcasts, "Real Christianity" and "King's Way Sermons." He resides with his wife and four children in a peaceful corner of the Arizona high country.

Church: KingsWayBible.org
Ministry: Relearn.org
Twitter: @DalePartridge
Instagram: @RelearnHQ
YouTube.com/RelearnTV

Shop.Relearn.org

OTHER TITLES BY DALE PARTRIDGE

———

AFFIRM YOUR CHILD'S
GOD-GIVEN GENDER

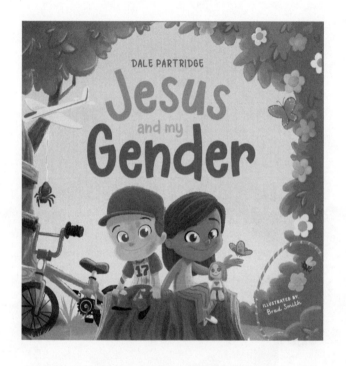

Relearn.org/Gender

AN INTRODUCTION TO THEOLOGY

Relearn.org/Theology

HEADSHIP &
HEADCOVERING

—

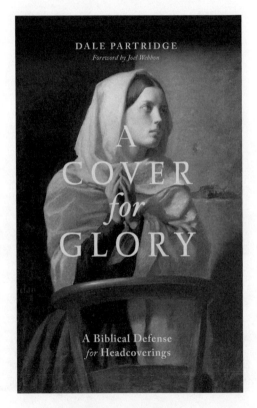

Relearn.org/Glory

LEARN BIBLICAL
MANHOOD

—

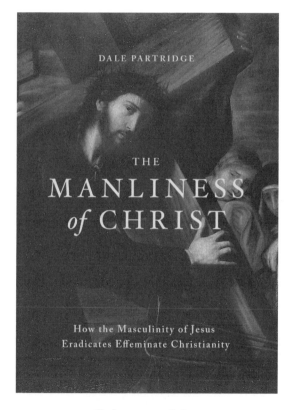

DALE PARTRIDGE

THE

MANLINESS
of CHRIST

How the Masculinity of Jesus
Eradicates Effeminate Christianity

Relearn.org/Man

READ OR MAIL
THE GOSPEL

A Simple Presentation of

THE
GOSPEL

A MESSAGE
of LOVE

FINDING FORGIVENESS, FREEDOM, & FAMILY

MailtheGospel.org